T0208276

Just Tell the Truth

A Narrative History of Black Men Told From The Inside

Cliff Harrington

iUniverse, Inc.
Bloomington

Just Tell the Truth
A Narrative History of Black Men Told From The Inside

iUniverse books may be ordered through booksellers or by contacting:

iUniverse
1663 Liberty Drive
Bloomington, IN 47403
www.iuniverse.com
1-800-Authors (1-800-288-4677)

ISBN: 978-1-4620-0949-7 (sc)
ISBN: 978-1-4620-0951-0 (hc)
ISBN: 978-1-4620-0950-3 (e)

Printed in the United States of America

iUniverse rev. date: 07/29/2011

CONTENTS

FOREWORD

"I will trust in the Lord. I will trust in the Lord. I will trust in the Lord. I will trust in the Lord until I die."

-- Negro Spiritual

The spirit of the ancestors has the power to baptize us in an everlasting river very much like the spicy waters from Dockery's pond. Not only does this spirit represent a culture that is unique to each one of us, it becomes a culture that resurfaces at any moment, especially when it comes to remembering the "Gathering of Old Men." Thus, the spirit of the ancestors lives on in me, and many others like me who are not able to, or were not able to transcribe into an intellectual context, the written words necessary to document such a vernacular into published volumes. Culture can be a curious thing. It can help to define us, and through its corridors, others discover where we stand on certain issues, how important we seem to be, and most importantly – how our world view has become tainted by what we have experienced. It becomes our script – our story – very much like the saga in William Shakespeare's tragedy, "Hamlet."

With the development of this "script" in mind, how then does one compartmentalize these ideas, experiences, and stories, into what we see as the message from the "Folks." (Folklore) Aristotle, Plato St. Augustine, other scholars and philosophers have grappled with these concerns, as I am in this current volume of words. I am yet challenged with the same kinds of dilemmas. How do I give justice to the legacy of these old men?

For example, Aristotle claims that Plato's arguments lead one to conclude that entities (such as anything man-made) and negations of concrete ideas could exist - such as non-good in opposition to good. This contradicts Plato's own belief that only natural objects could serve as standards of knowledge. Also, Aristotle refutes Plato's belief that Ideas are perfect entities unto themselves, independent of subjective human experience. Ideas, Aristotle claims, are not abstractions on a proverbial pedestal but mere duplicates of things witnessed in ordinary daily life. The Ideas of things, he says, are not inherent to the objects in particular but created separately and placed apart from the objects themselves. Thus, Aristotle says, Plato's idea that Ideas are perfect entities, intangible to subjective human experience, is meaningless, for all standards are based somewhere in ordinary human activity and perception.

Whereas, this volume by no means, has as its purpose, a philosophical analysis of culture or vernacular; I must give homage to the work of the aforementioned scholars as a launching pad for my inspiration – VOICES of "The Old Men". These men symbolize ideas of good, versus non-good, ordinary versus unordinary, secular versus non-secular-a means of producing their very own standard for knowledge.

In the 2001 publication of The African American Heritage Hymnal the lyrics of the Gospel Jubilee Song, "I Will Trust in the Lord" are published. Ironically, the preface line that is printed directly beneath the title of this song read as follows: 'In God, whose word I Praise, in God I trust; I am not afraid; what can flesh do to me? (Psalm 567:4) – reminds us of a commitment to one's inner faith. And this song that became the insignia of ritual for Wednesday night's prayer service became the true philosophical impetus for the folks to survive and truly believe a better day was coming. These believers had no need to be afraid, discouraged nor dismayed. After all, what harm could man bring them?

The lyrics of this song continue in this fashion:
Verse one: *I will Trust in the Lord.*
Verse Two: *I'm gonna treat everybody right*
Verse Three: *I'm gonna stay on the battle field.*

Journalist and Newspaper Editor, Cliff Harrington, is a graduate of the University of North Carolina, Chapel Hill. Thus, as a man of words, Harrington, as well as a veteran editor and newspaper writer has been given the spiritual privilege of peeking inside the bosom of this senior male population of whom he says 'treated him RIGHT!"

Thus, he returns the favor; he now treats these old guys right. He fulfills this favor by writing about them in narrative form, he recalls them.

Dr. Brooksie Harrington

Dockery's pond is like many other rural ponds that to this day are familiar because many people were baptized there.

DO WHAT YOU CAN, AND BE PROUD OF IT

I was a sophomore at UNC Chapel Hill. I went home one weekend for a visit. As usual, I attended church. One of the deacons walked up to me and handed me a quarter.

He said: "I don't have a whole lot to give you, but maybe as you're walking across campus on a hot day, you can take this quarter and buy yourself a soda."

He smiled and proudly walked away.

To this day, I wish I had held on to that quarter.

Chapter I

A view from the inside

I, Cliff Harrington, am in a strategic position to write this book about black men.

I am one.

I also am from the generation who grew in a time when there existed a strong faction of proud Black men who, at least in their communities, were respected.

My generation also knows that most black men are not the societal predators who, for decades, have been highlighted in newspapers, television and on radio.

I'm also a member of the print media. I've worked in newsrooms since 1977. I've been a reporter who gathered facts, and I've been an editor deciding what's covered, how it's written and where it plays in the newspaper. So I understand how the media can, and does, strongly impact the images buried in the public psyche.

Truth is that, in most cases, important information is born in newspaper newsrooms. Newspapers generally have had larger staffs and more skilled fact-finding abilities. While television and radio have, at least until the age of the internet, dominated the moment-to-moment news production, newspapers dominated investigations and deeper, quality reporting.

The phrase "strongly-impact" in an earlier reference is not necessarily a bad thing, or an indictment. In many cases, to most accurately tell a story, facts must be handled in a way that sets proper context and assigns appropriate weight to various facts.

That manipulation becomes negative when facts are maliciously or, through ignorance or conspiracy, used to move an audience away from the truth.

The media gives us facts and context to help readers determine what, or who, is good and what, or who, is bad.

In my career, I've sat in countless news meetings focusing on coverage of topics from racism to horse shows, and often I've inwardly struggled with discussions in which I was engaged. As a black man I've known and been proud of the culture in which I grew up. As an editor, I've known that my background was not familiar. I knew it was not lesser in value, just different.

I learned to live in two social realities to succeed professionally.

I was raised by a black man who stayed married to one wife, was dedicated to one family, worked hard and maintained his dignity in a world that said he couldn't. I grew up in a community where black men, the majority of whom worked hard, adhered to the tenets of Christian faith, respected women and demanded that we, as young men, adopt the approach that had sustained them.

It's not my aim here to devalue the role and history of black women. There have always been strong black women (read the biography of Ida B. Wells or, in a more recent era, Oprah Winfrey). In fact, black women proved to be more resilient than black men from the 1950s to the 1990s. Many black men in that period surrendered to ignorance, thereby helping society cast them in a role that should never have been theirs.

I also should state that this book did not adhere to the strict dictates of academic research. There is much of this work that can be substantiated through existing literature. And it is.

However, there are elements that can only be explained by one who lived among this group of black men, cam to understand them, their thought processes and behaviours, and subsequently came to love and respect them.

I did, and do to this day.

Now is the time that this truth can be told: There have always been good, strong, honourable black men.

The popular belief that black men would one day become extinct is a hysterical cry by those who know only what much of American society has propagated for the past century and a half. And during that period, many in society ignored the strong, honourable, wise black men.

Consider what James Baldwin wrote in 1963 to his nephew, James, in the book "The Fire Next Time:"

> *It will be hard, James, but you come from sturdy, peasant stock, men who picked cotton and dammed rivers and built railroads, and, in the teeth of the most terrifying odds, achieved an unassailable and monumental dignity.. You come from a long line of great poets, some of the greatest since Homer. One of them said, 'The very time I thought I was lost, My dungeon shook and my chains fell off.*

There was truth in Baldwin's words then and now.

I know.

I learned from black men who set high standards, and I remembered my lessons.

The black men I grew up around weren't perfect.

There were drunkards and scoundrels. But the stronger black men held enough impact in my neighborhood that the scoundrels both respected and feared the honourable black Men.

They were tough.

As a boy, I thought they were a bit mean. And often when my father went somewhere, I was with him. And I ultimately was around what I thought were a group of grumpy, boring old men.

They fixed things and shared knowledge about their skills. They worked hard, mostly as farmers, mechanics and builders. They believed, and taught the younger boys, that to be valued one must do work that leads to tangible results.

Their productivity sustained their family, so nothing made them waver from their work.

And the hard work sustained them. Many were physically fit well into the age of 70 or older. And medical care was not an option.

You didn't disrespect them because they were physically strong, many no more than two generations removed from the brutality of slavery, peonage and Jim Crow. So, they'd whip you if you did wrong. That's how they had been dealt with. At that time, I thought they were fully capable of killing.

Looking back, I now can see they had a gentle side, and frequently they were teaching us strength and self-discipline when they seemed harsh. They knew what my generation of black men would need to know, if we were to succeed.

You couldn't lie – and get caught. That was an automatic whipping.

You had to acknowledge them when they talked. That meant talking back respectfully, looking them in the eye.

You respected their homes. Many of the men didn't allow you to enter their home if you were drunk; and you didn't use bad language in front of women and children.

I can remember groups of teenage boys walking the rural road in the late evening where I grew up in North Carolina. We could hear them talking a quarter-mile away, but as they approached the yard when my parents were present, the tone and language became increasingly tame.

Attending church was required.

You might not participate after you got there, but you had to go. Black men ran, and in many cases still run, the church. Even today I marvel at how well-organized churches are, how they've endured, and how efficient they were with the money.

You learned to respect God first, then the authority of those men. They had their own ideas of justice.

When I was about eight years old, my dad caught a group of teenage boys outside our barn late one night. They all were from the neighborhood. He heard the noise, went out and confronted them, unarmed. I remember he told them to be back at our house the next morning... And I remember they all came back. I always wondered why they came back and what would have happened if they hadn't. My dad knew their parents, but, to my knowledge, he never told. They showed up, my dad gave them a stern lecture and sent them home. I still know and see many of those boys, now men. They weren't thugs or gangbangers. They were mischievous boys, bbut they understood and respected authority.

The justice system we know today would never have afforded them such mercy. They would have been hauled away in handcuffs and processed through what we accept as a criminal justice system.

Most of those strong black men from my neighborhood have died. And my old neighborhood, like many older predominantly African American neighborhoods, has been decimated by the drug culture and poverty due to the lack of jobs.

So the link between those men gets weaker each year. And as it has weakened, many in my generation have lost their identity.

The black men I grew up watching knew unequivocally who they were. And they didn't care how the world, particularly white America, perceived them.

They weren't fancy. I thought they were plain and unimaginative. Truth is they were so proud of their independence, that no amount of glamour or spotlight could make them change.

Yet, they understood the South, where slavery and peonage had dominated and racism still was as obvious as the grit and grease and dirt under their fingernails.

That grit and grease and dirt was there because of hard, honest work. The racism existed because of hard, selfish hearts.

To this day much of white America, and a good bit of black America, under values these older African American men.

And the men, themselves, are too proud to care.

If you want to see them, you must go where they are.

Though few in number, some still can be found. Just look for church leaders, teachers and principals, mechanics, doormen, and a host of other nonglamorus labourers.

The men I'm writing about were smart enough to know they couldn't change the world. They had lived through violence and difficult times, much of the violence aimed directly at them. So, they tried to teach my generation what they knew, give us their ethics of discipline and hard work, and hoped my generation would be the one that made this country different.

The way those men were perceived, and depicted in the media of the mid 60s, created a conflict for many young men of my generation. We were part of them and we knew they weren't all idiots, thugs, thieves and infidels.

Yet, we were so strongly attracted to riches, glamour and power, that many in my generation gave up the principles and conformed to a world that was less moral, poorly disciplined and consumed by making money.

The black men of my childhood did not abide debt and loans. You'll read more about that later. Those men lived within their means. That meant no one was rich. To some degree most were poor, but they had pride in what they owned.

I dare say Bernard Madoff would never have succeeded in taking their money. Those black men didn't have MBAs, but they held everyone accountable when it came to money. If they had been in positions of authority, the recession of 2008-09 would have been less likely because both lenders and borrowers would have been periodically required to give an account of how they were doing business.

It's ironic now that our first black President, Barak Obama, is being criticized for demanding accountability. Wise black men have long demanded it. Their demand for accountability was one of the traits that made them appear toughest.

My generation of black men grew up believing we would live a better life. And we do. And, many of us were able to hold to the lessons we were taught, even though it has put us in conflict with a world where those tenets didn't bring quick wealth and success.

We learned to survive in a white-male controlled world that defined us by their standards. The price we paid was that we redefined success, and the values of those old black men got watered down or washed away.

When people talk about "old school" black men now, they frequently are referring to the generation who grew up during the 1960s and '70s. They've forgotten there were times before that when black men were strong, wise and leaders in their home, neighborhood and across the nation.

That makes it even more ironic that successful black men have come full circle back to the values of the old black men who we, as young men, all too readily cast as out of step and irrelevant.

One of the men in the neighbourhood where I grew up was a builder. He built houses, built the church I attended until I left for college, and did other construction for people of all races. He was respected for his skilled work. He also was a Bible scholar.

Now, this may not seem exceptional until you know that he frequently made a point of telling us he had "a second grade education."

He wasn't bragging; He was exhorting us to get a better education. His theological knowledge was independent. I assume he got other knowledge while serving in the U.S. Army.

Still, he could quote scripture word-for-word. Sometimes we would have what we called "Missionary circle meeting" at various neighbourhood homes. He would lead. He would sit in one area of the room with no Bible. Direct us to turn to a scripture and read. Then before we could read, he would tell us what it said. And to my knowledge, he was never wrong. He was respected by everyone. He's no longer alive, but his teachings live on in all who spent time with him.

That includes me.

There is a Biblical parallel for the journey of many black men in America since the late 1950s. Read the books of Deuteronmy and Johsua. The children of Israel wandered 40 years in the wilderness.

Can you imagine being lost that long? Can you imagine walking in the same region, never realizing you're repeating the route to nowhere?

That's what many black men in America have done. We turned our backs on the principles of faith, due diligence and hard work. Many have forgotten, and some have lived their lives never knowing, that those principles sustained our fathers, grandfathers and great-grandfathers through slavery, Jim Crow, segregation, desegregation and even our modern era of corporate corruption, greed, self-indulgence and dishonesty.

Society has for nearly a century, spewed a pernicious venom about black men.

It's been published in print and broadcast on television and radio. In some cases, black journalists and leaders have done more to support the venom than raise voices of truth.

I frequently recall a phrase from my boyhood: "just tell the truth." You would hear that phrase when someone wanted to give voice to a point that may not have been particularly pleasant to listeners, or a point that had been conscientiously ignored. Well, on the topic of black men, it's time for all of America to "Just Tell The Truth."

The true meaning of Justice

Throughout my childhood, whenever adults would gather to talk, someone (man or woman) would, without failure, start quoting scripture.

Frequently, I didn't fully understand. But I did listen.

They would talk about sin, the 10 commandments and how there was no such thing as 'big sin and little sin. Any sin can send you to hell.'

That scared me.

And they always drew a clear distinction between what they called 'man's law' and 'God's law.'

I had to grow up to realize that they had an extremely sophisticated understanding of justice and ethics. And that understanding didn't waver based on any situation.

To this day, I've not found them to have been wrong.

CHAPTER II

THE ENDURING STRUGGLE

There is a concept of capitalism that says "whoever controls the means of production thereby achieves political domination as a ruling class" (Social Stratification: Class, Race and Gender in Social Perspective by Dave B. Grusky, P. 170).

That concept is significant in understanding a mindset that could lead to slavery, peonage, Jim Crow and constant image distortion, all aimed at black men.

Also, when you understand that concept of capitalism, it becomes more apparent that one of America's greatest conflicts was, and in many ways still is, between white men and black men. While that's not an absolute depiction, it is to a majority extent true throughout history.

The country's founding fathers wrote in the Declaration of Independence "We hold these truths to be self evident that all men are created equal. That they are endowed by their creator with certain inalienable rights…life, liberty and the pursuit of happiness."

Then they further reinforced that in the United States Constitution when they wrote:

> *"We the People of the United States, in Order to form a more perfect Union, establish Justice, insure domestic Tranquility, provide for the common defense, promote the general Welfare, and secure the Blessings of Liberty to ourselves and our Posterity, do ordain and establish this Constitution for the United States of America."*

With all that in place, the founding fathers proceeded over the next three generations to ignore those noble principles as they proceeded to satisfy their own greed.

The conflict has always been about wealth and power. In that struggle, the push for justice and morals became viable manipulation devices.

During Reconstruction, men of all races could vote. In fact, shortly after the end of the Civil War, black voters in some Southern states out numbered white voters.

It's also significant that women could not vote. That, for years, kept them out of the power struggle.

The ability to vote gave leverage to assign power and with that power one could assign wealth. Men of both races wanted the power and wealth. And black men were gaining, particularly in the South.

Hiram R. Revels of Mississippi became the first African-American elected to the U.S. Senate in 1870. He completed the term of former Confederate President Jefferson Davis.

That same year, Joseph Hayne Rainey became the first Black man elected to the U.S. House of Representatives. He was re-elected four times and had the longest tenure of any Black man during Reconstruction.

(Biographical Directory of the United States Congress).

Obviously those men got enough votes to be elected, and that tells you something about the electorate shortly after the Civil War. But the legacy of black men of wealth and power goes back even farther.

Before slavery black barbers had mastered the art of entrepreneurship. They made money and used it to help strengthen other black people.

Now, there also is a dark side to this history of black barbers. Some of them owned slaves.

But the barbers also taught many of the slaves to be barbers and formed a tight-knit society that, in many cases, supported other blacks and helped them get opportunities.

The story of William Johnson shows that the black barbers' legacy dated back to the 1830s. Johnson kept a diary of his life for many years. William L. Andrews wrote about that diary in the book: "William Johnson's Diary: The Text and the Man Behind It."

Andrews wrote that Johnson was the son of a slave woman and her master, and Johnson was given his master's name. Johnson went on to become a barber, and here is what Andrews wrote about him:

> *Barbering and hair dressing were vocations that free Negroes were allowed to pursue in early nineteenth century Mississippi and Louisiana, especially in the river towns of the delta. When he was 21 years old, William Johnson purchased the lease on his affluent brother-in-law's barbershop, along with… house and furniture, prior to the older man's move to New Orleans. A year before Johnson began his diary in 1831, therefore, he had managed to establish himself as a businessman and property owner whose ready cash and reputation for largesse made more than a few white gentlemen of Natchez his willing debtors.*

Douglas W. Bristol Junior wrote in "Regional Identity, Black Barbers and the African American Tradition of Entrepreneurialism":

> *Black barbers fended off white competitors by preserving the artisan system, inventing first-class barber shops, and catering to the racial stereotypes of their white customers. Of these elements, the artisan system formed the cornerstone of the black barbers' tradition of enterprise. It ensured work and decent prices for all through a system that took care of barbers from the moment they entered the trade until their death. Graduating through a series of reciprocal*

relationships, barbers started out as apprentices living under the roof and supervision of a master barber until they were eighteen or twenty-one. The frequency with which black barber shop owners took apprentices and the care they provided for their wards exhibited a commitment to mutuality.

In exchange, the elder barbers not only secured inexpensive help in their shops, but they also maintained high levels of skill and limited competition by controlling entry to the trade. Barber shop owners looked out for journeymen barbers as well, taking them into their homes, allowing them to court their daughters, and helping them become barber shop owners. These bonds of mutuality grew out of the African American community, with relatives, neighbors, and fellow church members of barbers arranging to have their son become an apprentice. Held together by such mutual care and respect, the fraternity of black barbers functioned like a medieval guild that established a virtual monopoly over the upscale end of the trade.

Black men, therefore, built a mode of commerce, in an atmosphere, that was determined to limit their social and economic mobility. And they prospered.

However, white men were not going to allow black men to control a town, a county, a region or any part of this county.

So, slavery dominated.

That did not end barbers work, it redefined who was in control. Then came the turn of the century and Peonage, but barbers still endured.

Eventually, the clientele changed from white men to black Men, but the barbers have endured and to this day hold a special place in the social network of the African American Community. There have even been movies produced about black barber shops – a way to show the value and legacy of this under-appreciated group of craftsmen.

They are evidence of a consistent thread that weaves deep into American history. Even as the forces against them grew stronger, black men endured as good businessmen.

Control via the justice system

For generations we've heard the phrase "institutionalized racism" and cast the term off as nebulous and unprovable.

However, the United States Justice system, while not formally racist, has had laws enacted that makes conditions favourable for racism.

Supreme Court Chief Justice Morrison Waite was among the first to galvanize racist behaviour into formal law. Immediately after the Civil War, his court dealt head-on with the impacts of the fourteenth and fifteenth amendments, which respectively afforded black people the rights of citizenship and the right to vote.

Waite was considered a benign, obscure selection when President Ulysses S. Grant named him Chief Justice of the U.S. Supreme Court in 1874. Some of the sitting justices even questioned his aptitude to carry out such a high task. However, during his tenure, which lasted until 1888, his impact was far-reaching and long-lasting.

Waite was known as a devout Christian of high morals. He also was viewed as not uniformly against civil rights for African Americans. However, some of his decisions indicate he was a man of contradictions.

In his book "The United States Supreme Court: the pursuit of justice," Christopher L. Tomlins writes that:

> *Waite was chief justice from the time of Grant's second administration through the administrations of Rutherford B. Hayes, James A. Garfield, Chester Arthur and Grover Cleveland. These years represented a transition from the immediate post-Civil War preoccupations with Reconstruction and the fate of the former slaves to late-nineteenth-century concerns about the impact of industrialization on American life. There were already enormous pressures for a return to so-called normalcy, which meant ending federal control of Southern politics and federal protection for blacks.*

Waite's court rendered rulings that set the tone for dealing with African Americans, particularly men, for the next century.

Some examples:

- *In Minor v. Happersett (1875) Chief Justice Waite declared for a unanimous Court that voting was not a privilege of national citizenship. Under the Constitution, states had the authority to regulate suffrage, and no one had ever previously suggested that states were required to give the vote to every person who was a citizen of the United States. The only change in this understanding brought about by the Civil War amendments was that states could no longer deny the vote based on race. (The United States Supreme Court: Pursuit of Justice, Tomlins).*

- *In U.S. v. Reese (1876) a unanimous Court declared unconstitutional sections 3 and 4 of the Civil Rights, or Enforcement Act of 1870, which made it a federal offense for state election inspectors to refuse to receive or count votes or to obstruct any citizen from voting. In his opinion for the Court, Chief Just Waite emphasized that under the Fifteenth Amendment, Courts had the authority to pass a law that addressed racial discrimination in voting but not to protect voting rights more generally, as the language of the statute seemed to do. Even though the prosecution alleged that the denial of voting rights was based on discrimination on account of race, the justices concluded that the foundation of this prosecution was a statute whose terms were overly broad. It was a fatal blow to federal protection of black voting rights. (The United States Supreme Court: Pursuit of Justice, Tomlins).*

- *U.S. v. Cruikshank (1876) was a case that made invalid a series of federal indictments alleging conspiracy to "injure, oppress, threaten or intimidate any citizens, with intent to prevent or hinder his free exercise and enjoyment of any right or privilege granted or secured to him by the Constitution of laws of the United States."*

(The United States Supreme Court: Pursuit of Justice, Tomlins).

That ruling came after a state militia of mostly black men had tried to occupy a courthouse during a political power struggle. The militia had been commissioned by the state's Republican governor. The militia was attacked by a mob of white men. Between sixty and a hundred black men were killed in what became known as the Colfax Massacre. Almost one hundred whites were indicted for violating section 6 of the Enforcement Act of 1870, but only a handful were eventually arrested and tried. Charges against that handful were ultimately ruled invalid.

In his opinion for the Court, Waite held that the rights at issue were protected against infringement by state and federal authorities, not against infringement by private individuals.

Because there was no indication that the defendants were acting as agents of the state, the federal government had no authority to intervene under the Civil War amendments; instead, the state governments had the responsibility of responding to acts of private individuals.

In her book, "The Colfax Massacre," author LeeAnna Keith wrote that after Wait's ruling: "…The campaign to reduce black political participation proceeded fitfully and painfully in coming years. The decisions in the voting rights cases Cruikshank and Reese had not disavowed black enfranchisement or even the federal obligation to prevent its obstruction. The ruling only limited the likelihood of intervention to prevent systemic abuses."

A few Republican papers warned that the gutting of the Enforcement statutes meant a new "opportunity for serious abuses, and perhaps terrorism in the South." (The United States Supreme Court: Pursuit of Justice, Tomlins).

(And that's what happened through random violence against black men and women, and through more organized action of the Ku Klux Klan.)

- *In Virginia v. Rives, Waite's court ruled that discrimination could not be assumed simply because no black jurors had ever been chosen in a particular county. As long as states were smart enough to enact formally neutral laws and judges smart enough not to declare that they were discriminating against blacks, the mere fact that no blacks were ever selected for juries would not be treated as a violation of the Fourteenth Amendment....*

(Hence, even today a jury of one peers, as called for by the U.S. Constitution, allows for a jury that may not include a person of the same race as the defendant. And while the concept has been strenuously argued, single-race juries happen frequently.)

- *From the beginning, the Waite Court had embraced a limited view of the power of the federal government to promote civil rights under the Civil War amendments. In many respects, then, the Courts infamous decision in the Civil Rights Cases (1883) merely represented a*

> *predictable culmination rather than an unexpected or dramatic departure. Still, the outcome carried with it the weight of history. (The United States Supreme Court: Pursuit of Justice, Tomlins).*

- *In an opinion written by Justice Joseph Philo Bradley, the Court declared unconstitutional the Civil Rights Act of 1875. The reasoning was entirely predictable, based on the results in Reese and Cruikshank: In the view of the majority, the Fourteenth Amendment was not designed to weed out discrimination by private individuals or businesses.*

- *Pace v. Alabama (1883) upheld a statute "imposing more severe penalties for living 'in adultery or fornication' when the parties were of different races." (The United States Supreme Court: Pursuit of Justice, Tomlins).*

Waite was very much in favour of states' rights and felt power should rest with state governments. He once was quoted as saying: "For protection against abuses by legislatures, the people must resort to the polls, not the courts." Waite also confirmed that "corporations would be considered 'persons' for the purposes of asserting constitutional protections under the Fourteenth Amendment."

The concept of corporate personhood is significant even today in the context of the theory that those who control the "means of production achieve political domination as a ruling class."

That concept allows the proverbial fox to rest calmly in the hen house. Corporations get to have extreme influence on our government and its citizens. Yet, corporations are bound by law to make money for their stockholders.

Hence, in some cases it's impossible for good governance and corporate interests to be reconciled. In cases where corporate and public interests are in conflict, corporations are better equipped to prevail.

Corporations have more money, more influence and are better organized. Public interest and good governance has suffered in many cases because of that.

Black men were not part of the power structure that established these basic foundations of how justice would meted out. Black men have been on the receiving end of the system. The modern-day face of the American justice system is quite diverse and execution of just treatment in most cases is carried out by men and women who's goal is the highest possible degree of justice.

Still, there are flaws that allow this system to fall short for a variety of reasons. And the people who most often get the harshest results are black men.

Oliver Wendell Holmes, in his book "The Common Law," wrote:

> *"The life of the law has not been logic; it has been experience. The felt necessities of the time, the prevalent moral and political theories, intuitions of public policy, avowed or unconscious, even the prejudices which judges share with their fellow men, have had a good deal more to do than the syllogism in determining the rules by which men should be governed. The law embodies the story of a nation's development through many centuries, and it cannot*

> *be dealt with as if it contained only the axioms and*
> *corollaries of a book of mathematics."*

Holmes' concept allows fluidity for laws to adjust to circumstance. And through that fluidity, the word justice, in many cases, became an absolute misnomer.

Legalized cruelty

Backed by a judicial system that tacitly and formally endorsed racist behaviour, white men proceeded to build their power base. After earning independence from what they perceived as an intrusive, domineering ruler in England, white men had become the "ruling class" of the United States.

White men controlled the economy and government from the beginning of the United States. They owned the land and the means of production – forced labour.

Slavery came first – free labor, today we'd call it low overhead. That was overt ownership of African Americans – men and women – and forcing them to work. The men proved to be physically strong workers who could, through mostly brutal coercion, be forced into high levels of production. Women also proved to be valuable, but, in most cases, in a more domestic arena. Black men became prized properties and were bought and sold like cattle.

When, in 1865, the 13th amendment made slavery illegal, a new system of forced labour, called peonage, gained momentum.

Peonage was a legalized system that allowed white men through a well-orchestrated governmental and penal system to control people who owed debts.

Black men were the target.

And Peonage was not a novel concept. It had been applied in other countries around the world. However, in the United States it was applied specifically to black people (most of its victims being black men) with the intent of getting free labour to power various money-making endeavours owned by white men. Hence, the victims were known as "peons."

That's another term that made its way into American vernacular and today people use it without understanding its history. Today many Americans wonder why black people, in general, and particularly black men, have such immense distrust for the United State's court system. You can find the roots in peonage.

Black men were the strongest and most productive labourers. Under the tenets of the peonage laws, a Black man could be arrested for anything from standing alone on a public street to talking too loud.

The arrest would result in fines, court costs, lawyers fees and other demands for money. When the man could not pay the demanded amount of money, he (again mostly black men) was imprisoned and forced to work. That meant going to whomever a judge chose and working there until the debt was deemed paid.

Frequently paying the debt took years, if not a lifetime. Many men died working in the harshest of conditions from the coal mines of the Midwest to the turpentine stills of the Southeast.

In the introduction of his book "Slavery By Another Name," Douglas A. Blackmon gives this account:

> *By 1900, the South's judicial system had been wholly reconfigured to make one of its primary purposes the coercion of African Americans to comply with the social customs and labor demands of whites. It was not coincidental that 1901 also marked the final full disenfranchisement of nearly all blacks throughout the South. Sentences were handed down by provincial judges, local mayors, and justices of the peace – often men in the employ of the white business owners who relied on the forced labor produced by the judgments. Dockets and trial records were inconsistently maintained. Attorneys were rarely involved on the side of blacks. Revenues from the neo-slavery poured the equivalent of tens of millions of dollars into the treasuries of Alabama, Mississippi, Louisiana, Georgia, Florida, Texas, North Carolina, and South Carolina – where more than 75 percent of the black population in the United States then lived.*
>
> *It also became apparent how inextricably this quasi-slavery of the twentieth century was rooted in the nascent industrial slavery that had begun to flourish in the last years before the Civil War. The same men who built railroads with thousands of slaves and*

proselytized for the use of slaves in southern factories and mines in the 1850s were also the first to employ forced African American labor in the 1870s. The South's highly evolved system and customs of leasing slaves from one farm or factory to the next, bartering for the cost of slaves, and wholesaling and retailing of slaves regenerated itself around convict leasing in the 1870s and 1880s. The brutal forms of physical punishment employed against "prisoners" in 1910 were the same as those used against "slaves" in 1840. The anger and desperation of southern whites that allowed such outrages in 1920 were rooted in the chaos and bitterness of 1866. These were the tendrils of the unilateral new racial compact that suffocated the aspirations for freedom among millions of American blacks as they approached the beginning of the twentieth century.

There now are countless reports worldwide of events surrounding slavery, the Civil War, Reconstruction, Peonage and Jim Crow. The purpose of this book is not to recount them, but put them in a context that shows how lasting the impact has been on black men and this nation.

Ralph Ginzburg, in his book "100 Years of Lynchings," has compiled episodes of lynching through the years. The book simply compiles various newspaper reports.

Many of the victims were hard-working, honest black men who were killed because they had amassed wealth and power. White men wanted the threat to their power base eliminated, so they lynched, burned, pillaged and took what they wanted.

Meanwhile, companies that had access to free labour (low overhead) flourished. Those companies became diversified industries and those industries gained legal personhood. Thus, they have controlled the nation's mode of productivity and therefore dominate the government.

With that structure soundly in place, the new goal became maintainance. How would those with the power, keep it?

So, a second strategy has played out over generations. A perpetual storm of media images, casting black men in a negative light, was heard, seen and given enough weight to obscure virtually any good black men did.

Trust yourself

Growing up, our water came from a spring we had dug in a nearby swamp. My dad, brother and I installed the pump and laid down the pipes that extended into our house. Sometimes, the pump would cease to function and no water would come from the faucet.

My father would walk down to the swamp, do some adjusting and yell for us to turn the water on. When there was water in the faucet he'd emerge from the woods.

One day when the water stopped. He walked down to the woods and returned a short while later. He hadn't asked us to turn the faucet on. When I quizzed him about it he said: "I knew what the problem was and I fixed it. I didn't need to check."

I learned that day that I too could trust myself and didn't need others approval, if I did the right things.

Chapter III

A Story with Consequences

It's no accident that the image of black men has been one that evokes fear, disrespect and disdain. And when black men are shown as successful, the reaction is skepticism.

Image manipulation dates back to the Civil War and Reconstruction.

Some highly-respected Southern newspapers, including The Atlanta Journal-Constitution, The Raleigh News and Observer, The Charlotte Observer were players. But they by no means were the only publications. Newspapers across the U.S. followed the pattern: Portray black men as unintelligent, lazy and sexual predators. Then draw the conclusion that they must be controlled, if not as slaves, then though the criminal justice system.

The media created a social enemy.

It was a long-lasting tactic that worked. The baggage of what history has done to the image of black men can't be denied even today.

Experts understand how much impact an image can have.

Shannon Winnubust in her book "Queering of Freedom" explains it this way:

> *"The Nike slogan 'Image is everything' captivates our faculties of judgment across the political spectrum ... This culture ran fixation with images is constantly read as indicating some state of grand transition – whether toward further decadence or more excessive liberation." (P. 60).*

What experts haven't assessed is how much this image distortion continues to weigh down American society – and particularly black men. Such an assessment would be difficult. Even today, in cases involving black men, when there are behaviours that allow room for interpretation, observers are left asking what would have been the reaction if the race had been different.

Here's a recent, familiar example:

> *In Summer 2009, Harvard scholar Henry Louis Gates Jr. arrived at his home after a long trip. When his door wouldn't open, he and an assistant forced it. A neighbour called the police assuming it was a break-in attempt. The neighbour did not identify the race of the person trying to enter the house.*

When a law enforcement officer arrived, Gates, who is African American, explained what was going on. The officer, who is white, entered Gates' home and demanded identification, which Gates provided. The professor showed the officer a driver's license and his Harvard identification. After that, things continued to escalate and Gates was arrested for disorderly conduct.

Gates says he was a victim of profiling, which simply means the law enforcement officer had a predetermined mental image of black men, how they acted and how they should be treated.

The officer says Gates was belligerent.

Profiling is a decades-old phenomenon whose existence many experts still debate.

As an isolated incident, reasonable people probably could argue the facts of the Gates incident either way. However, given the baggage of the American Criminal Justice System and black men, that incident took on heightened intensity. And we'll never know how the case would have been handled had the circumstances been different.

Images created by newspapers, television and radio helped set the tone for how black men are treated.

In 2006, The Charlotte Observer and Raleigh News and Observer published a special report on the Wilmington riots. In a jointly-published series, The Charlotte Observer and Raleigh News and Observer described in detail how their publications of the late 1800s help demonize black men and discouraged cooperative relationships between poorer white men and black men.

Again, in this context, it should be noted that before and after the Civil War and during Reconstruction, there were Black men with wealth and learning. Some were elected to public office. Others were educated, gained power and wealth. This all is chronicled in the book "From Midnight To Dawn."

The combination of violence and distorted images worked. Even black men and women bought into the "rotten black man" concept. And for generations, in many ways, it became a self-fulfilling prophecy that has tainted the minds of America.

The honourable Black Men of the 40s, 50s and 60s (and even many today), took on a demeanor that allowed them to survive. They became stoic, never allowing the outside world to know their thoughts or feelings. And they trusted only other black men – and that trust had to be earned.

Andrews in his book about barber William Johnson wrote this of Johnson's 1830s diary:

> *I want to introduce the tone and temper of William Johnson as reflected in his diary. I cannot promise a full portrait of this man, however, much as I would like to. A central obstacle to our knowing William Johnson as personally as we would like is his diary itself. Although we might expect the diary to be a*

*window into this man's heart, if not his soul, when
we peek into Johnson's diary we soon discover that
his window is heavily curtained. Only occasionally
does the diarist open the drapery of his privacy wide
enough to permit a look inside at the interior of the
man himself.*

More than 100 years later James Baldwin, in his book "The Fire Next Time," wrote to his nephew James:

*"Take no one's word for anything, including mine
— but trust your experience. Know whence you
came."*

As generations lived and died, knowledge of strong, productive black men has been replaced with images of men who are capable of accomplishing little, and are to be feared, loathed and controlled by a court system with a history of injustice toward them.

It's worth noting that even today, the criminal justice system leaves the door open to question how well it dispenses justice. The American Civil Liberties Union, in early 2000 revealed findings from a study that showed when the victim is white and the suspect is black, the black defendant is almost three times more probable to get the death penalty. That probability dramatically falls when the victim is black and the suspect is white.

Today there are countless cases of defendants released from prison and even death row, a large percentage being black men, who have been found to be unjustly or erroneously convicted.

Again, we'll never know how sincere the effort was to obtain justice. But we do know that the justice system has a history of being manipulated based on a variety of situations, Oliver Wendell Holmes himself said that earlier in this book.

The success of black men worried white men, particularly in the unstable South where people were working to regain power and wealth. White men turned to violence and scare tactics, and the courts did virtually nothing to stop it.

Probably one of the most significant examples of this violence, though by no means the only example, is the Wilmington Riots of 1898. Again, The Observer and News and Observer series of 2006 gives great detail about the surrounding circumstances.

For many years it was a story that had not been told. Racist violence in what then was the state's largest city destroyed a base of what had become a political and economic success story among black people.

The target? Black men.

And that violence sent a message across the nation. That could happen because the U.S. Supreme Court had earlier set the tone by its ruling in the Colfax Massacre.

According to the 2006 series:

> *"In the name of white supremacy, this well-ordered mob burned the offices of the local black newspaper,*

murdered perhaps dozens of black residents — the precise number is not known — and banished many successful black citizens and their so-called "white nigger" allies. A new social order was born in the blood and flames, rooted in what The News and Observer's publisher, Josephus Daniels, heralded as "permanent good government by the party of the White men."

A Just Reward

I've seen farmers prepare fields, plow fields with a mule, spread fertilizer by hand, plant seeds by hand over acres of land, and then wait.

They waited for rain. They vigilantly pulled weeds.

They waited for seeds to emerge as plants, plants to mature and vegetables to emerge. I never heard them complain.

It was understood: You go from labour to reward, and the journey is neither short nor easy. But there will be a reward.

Chapter IV

The psychology of dominance

There is a time-worn cliche in the South: "I'd rather struggle under a white man than be beholden to a black man."

That mindset cuts to the core of what many in our society believed in the past – and even today. The sentiment was born out of racism. Then as image distortion took hold, the sentiment came from the belief that black men really were inferior and, therefore incapable, of independently doing anything that was relevant and good.

That mindset allowed many in America to cast as less relevant the accomplishment of George Washington Carver, the scientist, botanist, educator and inventor. It's why we don't appreciate the accomplishments of Benjamin Banneker, a mathematician and astronomer.

History is filled with black men of accomplishment such as these.

There's also a second cliché from the South: 'slave's mentality.'

The phrase is used to describe one who feels inferior to a perceived master; a person unable to function without someone telling them what to do; only viewing oneself as good if you're defined as such by someone in a more dominant position.

Today we view that as a flawed psyche.

In the eyes of the older black men, there were clear definitions of what is good and what is right, and those definitions do not hinge on the judgment of people in power.

They hinged on Biblical tenets.

Many Black men who grew up in the early 1900s also understood that good and right had nothing to do with who held power over them. So they clung to a higher definition of good and right, and eschewed the society that gave them little chance to flourish.

However, there also is another form of flawed psyche. There is a negative side to domination.

Here's what George Mason said in 1773 at the Virginia Constitutional convention:

> *Slavery: . . . that slow Poison, which is daily contaminating the Minds & Morals of our People. Every Gentlemen here is born a petty Tyrant. Practiced in Acts of Despotism & Cruelty, we become callous to the Dictates of Humanity, & all*

> *the finer feelings of the Soul. Taught to regard a part*
> *of our own Species in the most abject & contemptible*
> *Degree below us, we lose that Idea of the dignity of*
> *Man which the Hand of Nature had implanted in*
> *us, for great & useful purposes.*

And in the 20ᵗʰ century, James Baldwin wrote these words (to his nephew) in his book "My Dungeon Shook".

> *... (his nephew) James must remain free of racial*
> *prejudice himself, however, in order to be clear-sighted*
> *in the fight against racists, for they are themselves*
> *frequently "innocent" and "well-meaning." He*
> *enlists his nephew's aid in making America "what*
> *America must become," that is, receptive to all of its*
> *native sons and daughters, allowing the black ones*
> *the same opportunities as the white ones."*

When any group has been dominant for generations, they come to believe there is no other way of life and therefore, those who who've been dominated are permanently cast in subservient roles. This, in the eyes of those who dominate, is right because they can't, or won't, perceive life differently.

There are four pillars of dominance, according to author and sociologist Philip Slater:

- *Deference or submission*
- *Systematic oppression through brutality and terror*
- *Deflection (creation of direct hostility toward others)*
- *Secrecy (A variety of secret codes, languages, symbols and systems used to keep the population ignorant.)*

Dominating a society has the practical impact of setting up an "us against them" mentality; it's the same as the mind-set of those who are being dominated. Once that polarization has taken place, you're not far from conflict and violence.

In the book "From Power to Partnership," author Riane Eisler writes:

> *"In the context of a dominator system, the basic assumption is that the way(to maintain the status quo) is to keep the have-nots under control and relatively poor. If they start getting things, they will presumably get things that the haves have ...*
>
> *"When confronted with the horrors of domination, we tend to assume the only way to make change is to match the dominators blow for blow, or even go one better ... when we take this stance, we are still acting, unconsciously, from the dominator paradigm, which says that we can only fight force with force."*

This has been lived out in U.S. history.

The civil rights movement was a dynamic push to change the mindset of America. It succeeded as laws were enacted or changed.

However, there still is evidence that there are people (in large numbers) in America who haven't moved beyond a mindset that says black men still should be dominated and controlled.

Code words and secret messages have been used even in modern times to ignite racist feelings and maintain a dominant power base. One classic example is the 2006 senatorial race between then-incumbent Sen. Jesse Helms and former Charlotte Mayor Harvey Gantt.

A hotly contested race pivoted, in a significant way, on a television ad many today identify simply as the "hands" ad. It showed the hands of a white man crumpling a job rejection letter. A voice in the background says the man lost the job to a "minority" because of racial quotas.

The implication is that the job went to a lesser qualified black man because of a government mandate to include people of color, and that something was taken that rightfully should have gone to the man who was rejected.

There is no discussion of qualification and fairness. It's simply implied that the job was unfairly taken from a white man.

The ad struck a nerve and polarized the senatorial race along racial lines. Helms kept his position as a powerful conservative voice. "Quotas" came to be an accepted term meaning something would be taken from a white person and undeservedly given to a black person.

A trait of conservatism is their passion for maintaining the status quo, keeping the power base in tact. That power base links directly back to the structure that has dominated America.

That power base was created in large part through economic advantage fostered in many states on the labour of black men. And that economic advantage has been parlayed into political savvy and control of the government.

For decades the prevalent discussion is how can black men be rehabilitated and incorporated into existing society in an acceptable way. Shouldn't there also be a discussion of how to rehabilitate the mindset of dominant society and how it can fairly relate to the good, respectable black men?

Black men were not wanted in the conversation when this country picked the various "means of production" because one of the stated 'means' was black men.

Today generations of young black men believe there only role in life is that of an outsider. And the images they see reinforce that in print, on television and radio.

A second, unspoken consequence is a society still rife with people who don't understand that some of what they perceive about race and race relations is based on lies fabricated and perpetuated toward a malicious end – harm black men.

We've spent decades constantly reporting and broadcasting the woes of a minority of America's black men and we've failed to cast that in the context that there has always been a stronger element of good and honorable black men.

It's no surprise at the number of angry, frustrated black men who believe there is no other path for them except crime, drugs, womanizing and ultimate death. This is not a problem that was created solely by black men. However, black men themselves ultimately must fix their mindset and thereby solve the problem.

Don't Lose Focus

As a boy, I frequently watched carpenters at work. I was always amazed at the precision with which they hammered nails.

It was almost rhythmic. Three, no more than four, light taps to start the nail. Then four or five more powerful thrusts and the nail was in.

They didn't waste energy or nails.

The arm was raised in precisely the same motion each time, and the hammer hit squarely on the head. The nail didn't waiver. The motion didn't waiver.

The nail went straight.

In fact, they were angered if a nail bent. I learned that they were extremely focused on that minute task. I learned to hammer a nail that exact way.

CHAPTER V

A STORY YOU CAN COUNT ON

Starting in the 20th century and continuing into the 21st, there is one story you can expect at least once a year to see on TV, read in newspapers and magazines, and hear on talk radio.

The story's premise: "There is a problem with black men in America." Then, the implied question to larger society is "How can we fix black men?"

The litany of articles, broadcasts and telecasts go like this:

- *More and more black men are locked in jail.*
- *Fewer and fewer black men are going to college.*
- *Young black men are turning to drugs, gangs and violence.*
- *Black women can't find suitable mates of the same race.*
- *And, the most extreme lie of all, young black men are becoming extinct.*

Trained journalists are taught in college that stories must have facts and context. Facts are what's real and, in a news context, often immediately in front of us. Context is the information that helps us understand how facts, and news, evolve and what the facts mean.

How much context you get in a given story, produced by any medium, is determined by time and space. The less time for a broadcast or the smaller the news hole, the less context you'll get.

Context also is determined by the writer's and editor's, or broadcaster's and producer's, judgment. Readers, viewers and listeners get the information writers, editors, broadcasters and producers agree should be published. If there are gaps in their knowledge or biases in their judgment, readers, viewers and listeners, in most cases, will never know.

And the other media reality is that they're businesses, and therefore must attract audiences. Most readers, viewers and listeners stick with written articles, telecasts and broadcasts as long as there is news. When the context kicks in, readers reflexively call it "rationalizing" and therefore move to something else.

The sad fact is that too much of what has been written, broadcast and telecast about Black men has been factual. Black men, to a great degree, have been hammered over and over with the facts they gave the media. And, the media has been all too happy to swing the hammer.

Many black men have robbed and murdered. Many Black men have raped. Many Black men have disproportionately participated in a drug subculture that has weakened them as individuals and the black family structure. Many black men have abandoned their children. Many black men have abused their wives. Many Black men have not valued education.

Many black men also have been wrongly arrested, tried, convicted and even sentenced to death.

While we face these facts, let's not lose sight of other facts. Having committed those crimes makes them no different from men of other races who, by the thousands, committed the same attrocities. And, by no means, should any man of any race be excused for crimes, sins or any such bad behaviour.

Still, there is missing context, particularly in the case of black Men. Here is an example based on the 2001 U.S. Census:

> *The U.S. Census says, there were 36 million African Americans in the United States. Just over 17 million of those African Americans are males, census numbers show. Figures from the U.S. Department of Justice numbers show that in 2009 there were close to 500,000 Black men in prison. The justice report also says the rate of imprisonment for black men was 3,161 per 100,000 people in the U.S. The imprisonment rate for white men was 487 per 100,000. The imprisonment rate for black women was 149.*

These Department of Justice statistics don't include the countless black men who are local or state jails, on a road to destruction, or, whose lives have been tainted because they've passed through what we accept as a criminal justice system. However, that's also not reflected for white men or black women. Still, it's safe to assume there are millions of black men living honourable lives, striving to be good men, good fathers and productive citizens. We don't hear much about them.

The single number, 500,000 is disproportionate.

And that means there has been validity in writing doom-toned articles about black men – sort of in the sense the media writes about the one plane that crashes and ignores the thousands that land safely each day.

The difference is that most of America assumes, and with good reason, that the vast majority of planes that leave the ground will land safely. Since slavery, there hasn't been any mass assumption that black men could and would do well in American society.

However, the facts show they have.

The 500,000 men in prison show roughly 3 percent of the whole picture of Black men in America. What hasn't been put in proper context is the many black men who have lived to a higher standard.

A more balanced report would have helped the public understand why there is a conflicted relationship between American society and black men. The message would have been that, while there are serious problems that must be addressed among black men, there also is inherent good, honour, courage, high morals and patriotism. And America has problems it also must address.

When the big story is the drug culture, there have been countless organizations of black men, reaching out for decades. Go to any city, find a long-standing black social organization or fraternity and you'll find a formal effort that has stood for years. One such example is 100 Black Men of America. They started their mentoring of young black men in 1963. They are not the only such example. In the era of gangs, there again have been many black men interceding. One of the most prominent is former NFL star Jim Brown.

And then, there are the older black men themselves, on which this book is based, – men who experienced World War II, the Korean War and the height of racism in America.

They laboured quietly, tried to be role-models in a society that said they couldn't, and tried to deliver a message to a group of younger men who chose not to listen. Their methods of delivering the message weren't always gentile and palatable, but they stood firm.

The media has mostly missed the bigger picture. Many good reporters understand something is going on with black men. When they wrote about the positive activities, the tone was of surprise and awe, when it should not have been.

Examining a fuller context would have made it less surprising to some segments of society, black and white, that in the 1960s Dr. Martin Luther King would start a movement that ultimately would transform the psyche for many in America, or that Thurgood Marshall could become the first black man named to the U.S. Supreme Court. Or that Bill Russell would become the first black coach in the NBA and that league's first black coach to win a championship, or Arthur Ashe could rise to the highest ranks of professional tennis in 1975 (a sport that for years was viewed as only for white people).

It also would have been less of a surprise that in the 1980s, Dr. Clifford Wharton Jr. would become the first Black Man to be named president of a predominantly-white university, Michigan State. Or that Alex Haley would write a compelling book titled "Roots," that would captivate much of a nation for a week as the series focused on African Americans' journey through slavery. Or that John Thompson would coach a major college basketball team to an NCAA title.

And with that as a backdrop, it would have been even less surprising that in the 1990s, Eddie Robinson would, for a while, become the winningest college football coach, at historically-Black Grambling State University. And he would do this while emphasizing the virtues of being an honourable man and holding himself as an example. He described himself as a man of one wife and a father to his children.

Or that, Tony Dungy could coach an NFL team to a Super Bowl title in 2007 or that Barak Obama would become president of the United States in 2008.

And, ironically they stood on the same principles the old black men held. And today the landmarks continue.

So the media must face its journalistic shortcoming. Too often it has been reflex to tell a most-negative story and then talk glowingly about having met its investigative responsibility.

And the consuming public of all races have comfortably accepted the stories – pathetic black man meandering aimlessly through a society they don't understand and, therefore, can't navigate.

Here's another classic example, which stands even today, of a distorted image.

Most people are familiar with the phrase "Uncle Tom" as an insult hurled at a person who betrays his African American cultural ties.

Depending on which version of history you read, and believe, the term "Uncle Tom" should never have been associated with dishonour. Harriet Beecher Stowe, who wrote the book "Uncle Tom's Cabin," has described Tom as a "…gentle, intelligent, religious and courageous black man." (From Midnight to Dawn by Jacqueline L. Tobin). Stowe's book was written in 1852 and the character, Tom, is believed by many to have been patterned after a strong, educated, courageous black man she knew.

In Tobin's book she writes:

> *Stowe's depiction of black people challenged prevailing myths about them. But her honesty was met by a resistant culture. Minstrel shows, with white actors in black face portraying blacks, had already become popular, especially in the North.*
>
> *'Tom Shows' were written with actors interpreting some of the more dramatic scenes from the book. .. Thus the character of Uncle Tom, written by Stowe to represent a noble black man, a Christ-like figure, was diluted to reflect the racist views of the times. Uncle Tom on stage became a shuffling, grinning black man who would do anything to ingratiate himself with whites. The term 'Uncle Tom' was coined; a slur used to define blacks who would demean themselves and their culture for the approval of whites..."*

This is a bit of history that, like so many other bits, has been conscientiously ignored or, even sadder, never taught in our schools.

That leads to another sad truth.

Too many Black journalists lack the perspective to make things different. They know only what they've lived and been told. And that doesn't include this deeper, richer story.

Most newsrooms still are largely run by white men. A study by the University of Georgia's James M. Cox Jr. Center for International Mass Communication Training and Research found in 2007 that minorities (anyone who is not white) were hired at a slower rate in U.S. newsrooms. In 2005-2006, roughly two-thirds of minorities who sought newsroom jobs, got them. And that was before the massive purge of 2008-2009, when a recession decimated many newsrooms and shut down others. Meanwhile, a little over three-fourths of White Americans who sought jobs in journalism were hired.

Finding media jobs has been tough for all trained professionals, but the statistics show it has been particularly tough for minorities. And as the recession hit the newspaper industry, the already-slender number of African Americans became fewer.

You're designated "minority" because there are fewer of you than other groups. Now, the hiring rate is slower. That formula simply perpetuates an already-existing problem.

You have seen more black men, and women, news reporters on television since the election of President Barak Obama. However, his leadership has not greatly impacted those in the newsrooms' decision-making chairs.

Fairness dictates that this truth also be known. Much of the leadership in today's American newsrooms is enlightened, well-intentioned, highly-skilled and professional. They produce credible media and they work extremely hard to present accurate reports, but more diversity could broaden the perspective.

A question of balance

I remember learning to change the tire on a car. It was explained to me that putting the lugs on a tire was a crucial task that should not be done arbitrarily.

The order is top, bottom, left, right. That makes sure the tire sets straight.

Lug tension should be equally distributed among the four until the tire is appropriately tight.

Not too tight, because you would have to take the lugs back off when you needed to change the tire. Not too loose because you risked the tire coming off.

The deeper lesson: No extreme, be it thought or action, will lead to a good end.

CHAPTER VI

THE DEPTH OF THE CONFLICT

In the mid 60s to early 90s, the mindset of Black Men simultaneously evolved and devolved.

Former slaves and men from the period of peonage (Generations born roughly from 1860 through 1950) first sought survival. They felt their self-sufficiency was their only refuge.

They had to have their own money, homes and methods of living, no matter how meagre. If it belonged to them, no one could take it or force them to give it up.

And their life actions were based in reality because many knew cases where black men had been murdered, imprisoned or mutilated. And the violence was due only to skin color.

The men who survived were tough.

They hid their emotions, guarded their homes and ruled with stern discipline. They pushed their sons, and daughters, toward a day when life would be different and, they hoped, better.

They shared a common bond, it became known as "the struggle." That phrase came to signify people who survived the rough times and continued to march toward social equality, fairness and justice. And there was pride in knowing one was part of the struggle.

That pride was shown through the afro hairstyles that started in the mid 60s and can be seen even today. Though today, it's mostly a fashion statement.

There also were those who wore African attire, a way of showing a link to Africa.

And one symbol that stood out was the raised clinched fist.

It didn't originate there, but the clenched fist gained notoriety in 1968 due to Olympic stars Tommie Smith and John Carlos, who displayed the symbol while standing on the platform after a victory. During that same time period, James Brown recorded "Say It Loud, I'm Black and I'm Proud."

To many, the song and symbol took on anthem-like meaning. It was particularly popular among black men. While the raised, clinched fist evolved into simply a clinched fist, it stood as a sign of pride in oneself and the brotherhood to which black men belonged.

Today it's still used universally as a sign of brotherhood.

And then there was use of the word nigger. No one really knows where the word, in the context of African Americans, originated. Maybe it originated for the Spanish word Negro, which means black. Or maybe it was just lazy pronunciation on the part of slave masters. Or maybe it was meant from the first time it was uttered as a derogatory name, aimed at demeaning.

The word has had legendary impact.

Black men uttered, and still utter the word, among themselves and openly.

Many say they have reclaimed it, and thereby taken the sting and hurt out of it. Still nothing positive has been born of its use.

Even in the 20th and 21st century, when the word is said – and it doesn't matter who utters it – the word bestows a kind of negative psychological hierarchy.

The person who utters the word has psychologically set himself, or herself, in a position of superiority and judgment, looking down on the person to whom they're referring. It's a word that communicates one's condescencion.

Think of the most frequently used sentences in which it's used:

"My ------."

"------ come here."

"He's just another ------'

Comedian Richard Pryor explained in the 1980s why he stopped using the word:

"I was sitting by myself (in the Nairobi Hilton in Kenya) and I just looked around and it was like a voice said to me ,"What do you see?" And I said, "People of all colors doing things together."

And another voice said "Do you see any niggers?"

And I said, "No!". And the voice said "Do you know why?"

And I said (whispering),"No". And it said, "There aren't any…"

He articulated an experience that gave insight into where racial equality must begin. Black men had to believe, amid all the harsh, conflicting messages, that they deserved to stand equal. That has taken time for some.

Pryor went on to say:

Black people should stop using the "nigger word" publically. It may take a longer time for some of us to stop using it privately and among ourselves, referring to ourselves, but it is a self-destroying word, demeaning ourselves to the level of our slave masters' concept of us as inferior and like animals.

It has taken generations for black men to see themselves as who they really are.

Some black men succeeded during the Jim Crow era. They had gone to colleges and universities.

Hence, their mindset shifted from simply surviving to challenging and competing. A college degree afforded the limited presumption, on the part of white America, of intellect.

A degree from a predominantly white university held a balancing effect. It awarded a presumption of intellect and an implication that, even though the skin color was different, that person would do things the way of mainstream America. And those ways, frequently, put black men in conflict.

There was the voice of the older black men, saying "you've got a chance......," "you can do things I never had a chance to do."

They also held firm to their strict Christian tenets.

While the younger black man saw wealth his parents and grandparents would never have, and all that came with it. And it was all there, through education. So they seized it.

Many black men came to believe that the way of white America was, indeed, the best way. They were persuaded that, if you worked hard enough in white-dominated, corporate America and played by some unwritten set of rules, you would obtain success and equality.

Many black men did indeed succeed.

They've made money, live elaborate lifestyles and have obtained a measure of power. Still, little has changed in the foundation of the corporate structure built centuries ago by men determined black men would never be their equal.

The major American Corporations in 21st century still are controlled, and largely run, by white men.

The term "soul brother" evolved to identify a black man who had learned the rules of white America, and played the game – without denying roots to his deeper, richer heritage. More and more black men dove into "mainstream America."

And, more and more turned their backs on the old tenets.

Over the years, America has gotten less racist, more accepting of all men and more inclined toward justice.

Still, a paradox exists.

Biases against black men have been so cemented that many in America still don't perceive black men as capable of competing for wealth and power, or leading a nation.

Since Barak Obama's election in 2008, a consistent theme has been articulated: "we've gotten away from our heritage and we're headed in the wrong direction.

The implied message being that a black man is not supposed to rise to such heights and does not have the wisdom to lead this nation.

In 2008, Senate Majority Leader Harry Reid, a democrat from Nevada, referred to then presidential candidate Barak Obama as "light-skinned" and speaking with "no Negro dialect, unless he wanted to have one."

Meanwhile, Rod Blagojevich, the ousted Illinois governor, said these words, referring to Obama in Esquire Magazine:

> *"... I'm blacker than Barack Obama. I shined shoes.*
> *I grew up in a five-room apartment. My father had*
> *a little Laundromat in a black community not far*
> *from where he lived. I saw it all growing up."*

While both men ultimately backed away from their comments and indirectly apologized, these statements show that there exists in their minds an image of what a black man should be.

While we're still not clear on the image those two men have, it's safe to conclude those images do not give due credit to black men's history of skillful articulation (read about Fredrick Douglass and W.E.B. DuBois) and afford a presumption of high levels of success (the success of the Black church and Black male barbers).

A 2008 documentary broadcast on HBO ("Right America: Feeling Wronged") focused on conservative white Americans and their reaction to the first black president. Many in the documentary did not say, or did not understand, that race was at the root of their feelings. To them, their social order had been violated.

Generations of white people have grown up being taught only to be faithful patriots and good, benevolent citizens. And they are.

However, being a faithful patriot also, in some crucial areas of society, has meant holding fast to the foundation set up by racist leaders hell-bent on harming black men. That foundation was laid generations ago.

Current generations have clean hands, except for an occasional racist statement, injustice or violence.

So, in today's America, a white person can say "I'm not racist" and "I've never done anything to you."

And they're most likely telling the truth.

Most are truly genuine and we of all races should embrace sincere, racial brotherhood.

But there still is an internal rot that allows racism.

It exists in the hearts of some men and in their ability to manipulate a structure that allowed cruelty and racism. It exists in their ability to maintain clean hands while they ignore the pain of others.

Black Men still receive the most harsh results when that plays out. And most often the umbrella of conservative politics is the portal through which evil enters.

Russell Kirk's book "The Conservative Mind," written in 1953, became the playbook for what many Conservatives believe even today.

Here are some highlights:

- *There is an enduring moral order: "That order is made for man, and man is made for it: human nature is a constant, and moral truths are permanent."*
- *Conservatives are persuaded that freedom and property are closely linked. Separate property from private possession, and Leviathan becomes master of all. Upon the foundation of private property, great civilizations are built. The more widespread is the possession of private property, the more stable and productive is*

> *a commonwealth. Economic leveling, conservatives maintain, is not economic progress.*

Even before the book was written, this Conservative mindset existed to the point that it could justify slavery and cruelty. White men viewed black men as naturally intellectually inferior and therefore to be used as laborers.

Kirk also wrote:

- *"The conservative adheres to custom, convention, and continuity. It is old custom that enables people to live together peaceably; the destroyers of custom demolish more than they know or desire. It is through convention – a word much abused in our time – that we contrive to avoid perpetual disputes about rights and duties: law at base is a body of conventions.*
- *Conservatives believe in what may be called the principle of prescription. Conservatives sense that modern people are dwarfs on the shoulders of giants, able to see farther than their ancestors only because of the great stature of those who have preceded us in time. Therefore conservatives very often emphasize the importance of prescription – that is, of things established by immemorial usage, so that the mind of man runneth not to the contrary. There exist rights of which the chief sanction is their antiquity – including rights to property, often. Similarly, our morals are prescriptive in great part.*
- *Conservatives pay attention to the principle of variety. They feel affection for the proliferating intricacy of long-established social institutions and modes of life, as distinguished from the narrowing uniformity and deadening egalitarianism of radical systems. For the preservation of a healthy diversity in any civilization,*

there must survive orders and classes, differences in material condition, and many sorts of inequality. The only true forms of equality are equality at the Last Judgment and equality before a just court of law; all other attempts at leveling must lead, at best, to social stagnation.

Hence, these tenets locked in place years before Kirk by Chief Justice Morrison Waite stand today as a foundation for our current paradigm of conservative politics and justice.

Law is based on judicial precedent. The conservative party clings to old ways, even as facts show those old ways are based in selfishness and racism.

Kirk also made clear the concept of why controlling the "mode of production" was linked to "controlling the government."

- *Conservatives uphold voluntary community, quite as they oppose involuntary collectivism. Although Americans have been attached strongly to privacy and private rights, they also have been a people conspicuous for a successful spirit of community. In a genuine community, the decisions most directly affecting the lives of citizens are made locally and voluntarily. Some of these functions are carried out by local political bodies, others by private associations: so long as they are kept local, and are marked by the general agreement of those affected, they constitute healthy community. But when these functions pass by default or usurpation to centralized authority, then community is in serious danger. Whatever is beneficent and prudent in modern democracy is made possible through cooperative volition. If, then, in the name of an abstract Democracy, the functions of community are transferred to distant*

> *political direction – why, real government by the consent*
> *of the governed gives way to a standardizing process*
> *hostile to freedom and human dignity.*

Comedian Bill Maher, host of an HBO talk show has been quoted saying "all Republicans aren't racist, but if you're a racist, you're probably a Republican."

Kirk's principles, while many are not racist when read literally, allow racists to flourish through interpretation and offer what sounds like sound reasoning. Though Kirk didn't live during slavery, he had to be familiar with Jim Crow.

The principles he wrote left the door open for inclined people to work together against black people. And again, black men have suffered most.

Twenty-first century Republicans aren't purely racist, and 21st century Democrats haven't wholly embraced racial equality. However, it's the conservative movement whose actions have shown how racist behaviour can be justified by conservative thinking, from Jesse Helms' and Strom Thurmond's segregationist push of the 20th century to Joe Wilson's precedent-setting shout of 'you lie' during a presidential speech by Barak Obama.

From Justice Waite's rulings to Kirk's writings, little about the foundation has changed. The truth lies in the execution of their words.

There are more nuances today. And men of honour and good-will have prevailed in making America more just and fair to everyone.

Still, those who cling to the conservative ideology don't understand why generations of black men are at best wary and distrustful, and at worst resentful and seeking revenge.

Conservatives simply see black men who are despondent, angry and uncommunicative. And the question becomes "what's wrong with them?".

A large number black men who became elderly during the 20th century, accepted only one moral code – the Bible's 10 commandments. It was what they had been taught and it's mostly what they handed down to their sons.

Hence, their intolerance for lying, their demand that you attend church, their requirement that you work *hard*, and have something to show for your labour.

And this background is why they are skeptical, even now, of "mainstream America," where daily practices of corporate America and Biblical teachings, frequently are at odds.

Black men, who remembered the harsher times, had no tolerance for variance, when it came to Biblical right and wrong. And they taught those who would come after them that veering into a world of selfishness and greed would lead to destruction. And the destruction they described looked very much like the recession of 2007-2008, or worse.

Many didn't listen to the teachings. Others viewed it as out of step and antiquated.

Today, the wisdom is obvious.

Reliable

In rural North Carolina where I grew up in the '60s, baptisms were held in "Dockery's pond," referenced at the beginning of this book.

The baptisms were held in early fall and people dressed in a nearby building that I don't remember much about.

I was baptized there in that pond. I remember the water was cold and the room where I changed didn't have a light.

I do remember there was a routine to the baptism. One man would take a tall pole and walk out into the pond.

He was the first in the water, and he went alone.

When he got to the appropriate depth, he would push the pole into the ground to mark the spot where the preacher would stand.

I was always intrigued that the same person took the pole out and marked the spot, and everyone trusted his judgment.

There was never a mishap.

And that may have been one of my first lesson in trustworthiness.

Chapter VII

The myth of 'Acting White'

However, the sons of the black men who witnessed legalized cruelty, injustice, violence and hypocracy, became blinded by their own anger and confusion.

There was anger at the history of unfairness that seemed to know no end. The frustration was, and in many instances still is, about voices who told black men who they were, and what they would become – criminals and vagrants.

And the voices were not their own.

So they turned against the voices and all that was associated with them. Hence, the "acting white" dynamic has played out in severe ways among black men during the 20th and 21st century.

In school, if a young black male was a student with good manners and study habits, he was ridiculed as "acting white." If he was all that, and chose to be sexually self-disciplined, he was "gay" and "acting white."

That made him subject to verbal and physical abuse from others of his own race. There was no middle ground. The student was cast into the role as a victim and his aggressors as thugs.

There was no option to simply be normal.

Truth is they all were in need of an accurate lesson about their heritage. That alone could have impacted their behaviour.

Many black men rejected the tenets of Christianity because they saw some older black men in neighbourhood churches as weak. They never took the time to understand why older Black Men often took the road of least resistance – translation: they didn't fight back.

They also failed to recognize that the African American Church has been one of the strongest institutions in America. The older back men played a key role in leading that by handling finances, securing loans, maintaining order and maintaining high morals.

And they did it in a society that mostly said they were incapable because they lacked the intellect. Still, African American History cannot be accurately told without including the church and many of the leaders in those churches were black men.

Were there scoundrels and predators in the churches?

Yes.

That story is frequently told – even today. But you also will find scoundrels and predators littering the history of Catholics and Fundamentalists.

Again, the difference is presumption. It's almost a reflex to presume the best for most faiths, and the worst when it comes to the African American Church.

And, another truth is the Christian church did become an institution for manipulation.

Slave masters used scripture to justify brutal beatings of black men and women. They used scripture to justify keeping a race of people subservient (Read Russel Kirk's tenet about natural order in the previous chapter).

White preachers offered sermons glorifying the happy-servant-status black men and women.

This was first noted by Fredrick Douglas in the 1840s when he wrote:

> *"We have men sold to build churches, women sold to support the gospel, and babies sold to purchase Bibles for the poor heathen! All for the glory of God and the good of souls! The slave auctioneer's bell and the church-going bell chime in with each other, and the bitter cries of the heart-broken slave are drowned in the religious shouts of his pious master. Revivals of religion and revivals in the slave trade go hand in hand."*

Douglas wrote that in 1845 in "Narrative of the Life of Fredrick Douglass, An American Slave."

So history has given reasonable black men a reason to mistrust, and even fear, the Christian religion. But that faith has given equal reason for trust and respect when you survey the list of civil rights leaders, and assistance services born in that faith.

And while many didn't know the complete history, they did see behaviour. They saw older black men whose experience and wisdom told them not to stand up to white men, no matter what the situation.

With limited understanding, younger black men labelled their seniors as cowards.

They saw white men with wealth achieved through the hard work of others. Younger black men came to believe this was the smart way. If you could make money and not work, why work?

In the span of a generation, it became easy to perceive education, justice and power as the domain of white America. That made it easy to resent anyone who behaved with the traits of white America, particularly if that person was black.

It also gave rational justification to black men who wanted an easy way to money and pleasure.

The drug and gang culture evolved in the African American Community, in part, as one way for a young black men to show the those around him that he was not "acting white."

Make no mistake about it, there were those black men who had no intention of doing the right thing. Drugs and gangs became their haven and they preyed on vulnerable, ignorant black men. They fell into that culture who thought "This is what we do. We have no other choices….."

They may never have known the older black men of honour and dignity.

By the late 60s and early 70s, younger men were too enamoured with wealth and pleasure. Doing the right thing, the right way had faded with the dying generation.

However, there is a faithful segment of black men you can find across America, and beyond. They're quietly navigating a changing society and trying to reconcile success, morals and peaceful coexistence in a society that still remains somewhat hostile.

Patriotism

I've known World War II veterans, Korean War veterans and veterans of Vietnam.

My saddest experience was linked to the war in Vietnam.

A young man from the neighbourhood where I grew up was killed there. I remember the tears of his mother, father and sister. I remember the chilling sound when the guns blasted a three-round salute at his grave side. I remember the painful drone of taps being played by a soldier who stood behind a tree about 100 yards away.

I also remember seeing other war veterans stand at attention, saluting as the flag was flown.

"That's what you're supposed to do," they said.

No questions asked. It was expected.

So was patriotism.

CHAPTER VIII

UNDERSTANDING AND RECLAIMING

In the 21st century it's not news that black men are successful, educated subscribe to high morals, and want their stake in a society their forefathers helped build.

Black men have fought in all the wars, starting with the Revolutionary War. Many are familiar with Crispus Attucks, but did you know thousands of black men fought in the Revolutionary War?

Black men fought for the Confederacy and Union in the Civil War. In recent years, many black men who fought for the Confederacy have been honoured as Civil War heroes. However, it still is awkward in many parts of the country to talk about that issue, even though records show black men received pensions for fighting for the Confederacy.

Black men helped build the country.

Slave and forced labour created wealthy men in the South and throughout the country. And those men parlayed their wealth into political power and control.

Today the grandchildren, great-grandchildren, and even great-great-grandchildren from many of those families still are tied to the wealth and power.

So the news now ought to be that there is a paradigm shift.

To borrow a sports analogy, a playing field that had been severely swayed to hinder black men, now is tilting toward a more level state were all men who are willing to work, and are of good intent and character can achieve some success.

Actually, professional sports (many of which have large numbers of black men playing) may be showing us how psychology has shifted toward equality.

Professional athletes aren't bad men because they withhold their services until they're satisfied with the contract they receive. They are simply playing by the rules of American capitalism. They're controlling the "mode of production."

Now, capitalism and ethics are at odds on the basic concept of a contract.

The obvious fact is that when you've signed a contract, you've given your word in writing that you will do something. Black men from the late 19th and early 20th century put extreme stock in that. "A man's word is his bond," they would say.

In our capitalist society, it has become accepted behaviour to agree to, and sign, a contract, and then abandon it before the terms have been carried out by the parties involved. We rationalize that behaviour simply as a "change in situation."

The stricter black men from the late 19th and early 20th century would have said "you lied."

It is true in this 21st century, the business atmosphere is dramatically different from 100 years ago. Laws have skewed businesses away from their orientation toward doing the right thing. They're obligated by law, and driven by greed, to make more and more money. Few options are left for workers who also are driven by greed, but may seek basic fairness for their wares.

In the case of professional athletes, it's their bodies that create the athletic prowess the public is willing to pay to watch. The public, impressed by what athletes do, then want to wear the clothes athletes wear, drive the cars athletes drive, drink the drinks athletes drink and consume a host of other products endorsed by athletes.

Product vendors are willing to pay these athletes to endorse various wares. And athletes willingly become salesmen. They gain from their jobs and their endorsements.

So why wouldn't a wise athlete seize control? It all starts with them.

That doesn't make him or her selfish; It makes them wise business people.

Sports and entertainment early on provided the opportunities where African Americans, particularly black men, could gain financial footing in society. They could gain wealth, control production and earn respect.

Consider the old Negro Leagues baseball teams, the "Chitlin' Circuit," for black performers, the popularity of Motown in the 1960s, many areas of the gospel music industry from the 60s until present, and a host of other arenas where black performers get opportunities.

Those arenas helped performers make a respectable living in a society that largely rejected them – until it became obvious there was money to be made.

The same quality of minds that helped create the Negro Baseball Leagues, Chitlin Circuit, Motown and other opportunities, now are sitting in board rooms, elected offices, classrooms, and other facets of life.

The intellect has been in our midst all the time.

Now, we have a clearer vision of this American asset known as black men. And that asset will be needed to build a brighter future.

The Million Man March of 1995 was a significant event because it allowed black men to see they are not exceptions when they try to do the right things. Fact is they were among a legion.

There were hundreds of thousands of men at that gathering in Washington, D.C., led by Nation of Islam (an opportunity the Christian Church missed when they didn't take more of a leading role).

The men of all faiths who attended saw other men like them – hard working, honourable and, yet, not quite aware of each other.

And, seeing that, black men became empowered to define themselves. They discovered they didn't have to live down to the images held up by inauthentic voices in the media and others who did not know them.

The march was not a gathering that invented honourable black men. They had always existed. It was, however, a gathering that shined a light on and, in many ways raised America's consciousness to, the legacy of black men and raised the possibility that a more truthful, richer story about them might someday be acknowledged.

The story has been told many times and in many ways. And each time the threads of honour, dignity and wisdom shone through. W.E.B. Dubois and Booker T. Washington were different in their approach, but they were consistent in the age-old message that had sustained black men throughout history.

They both were right about many things, each in their own way.

Listen to them nearly a century ago.

Washington said in his book "The Negro Problem":

> *No race can be lifted until its mind is awakened and strengthened. By the side of industrial training should always go mental and moral training, but the pushing of mere abstract knowledge into the*

head means little. We want more than the mere performance of mental gymnastics. Our knowledge must be harnessed to the things of real life. I would encourage the Negro to secure all the mental strength, all the mental culture – whether gleaned from science, mathematics, history, language or literature that his circumstance will allow, but I believe most earnestly that for years to come the education of the people of my race should be so directed that the greatest proportion of the mental strength of the masses will be brought to bear upon the every-day practical things of life, upon something that is needed to be done, and something which they will be permitted to do in the community in which they reside.

Dubois in his essays said of Washington:

"Mr. Washington represents in Negro thought the old attitude of adjustment and submission; but adjustments at such a peculiar time as to make his programme unique. This is an age of unusual economic development , and Mr. Washington's programme naturally takes an economic cast, becoming a gospel of Work and Money to such an extent as apparently almost completely to overshadow the higher aims of life….Mr. Washington's programme practically accepts the alleged inferiority of the Negro races. … In the history of nearly all other races and peoples the doctrine preached at such crises has been that manly self-respect is worth more than lands and houses, and that people who voluntarily surrender such respect, or cease striving for it, are not worth civilizing."

Hence, there has always been value and honour among black men. It didn't matter whether they were farmers, carpenters, mechanics or doctors, lawyers and scientists. Black men cover the spectrum.

Their roles have not always been glamorous or in the spotlight. And generations have missed them, due either to rejection or ignorance.

Still, they've survived.

CONCLUSION

"Already the more far-seeing Negroes sense the coming unities: a unity of the working classes everywhere, a unity of the colored races, a new unity of men....A belief in humanity means a belief in colored men. The future world will, in all reasonable probability, be what colored men make it. "

W.E.B. Dubois,
The Essential W.E.B. Dubois Collection, 1897

This book is not written as a call to anger, resentment and violence toward any man.

There is now enough evidence ranging from the Civil War through Jim Crow, the Civil Rights movement and the advent of Affirmative Action to show that any remnant of ill will between men of any race is counterproductive to American society.

If we are to survive as a society, we need each other. And we must deal with each other in an honourable way.

So, the point here is that the story of black men long ago should have been heard as it was told from an inward perspective. We, as Americans, should abandon all the acts that are based on untruths and buried truths perpetuated for generations.

Black Men should turn to and embrace their history and an identity that has stood for centuries. That heritage is based on wisdom, honour, faith and hard work.

Settling for less is failure.

THE END

*This photo taken at Ellerbe Grove Missionary Baptist church in
the late 1930s or early 1940 shows a common scene of that time.
Many black men did live lives of dignity and love of their families.
Some how, history has forgotten these unpretentious men.*

In honor of:

James Stancil Harrington, Virgil McKay (Korean War veteran), Charles Mumford, Vea Martin.

In memory of:

James Harrington, Ben McCain, Tom Ellerbe, Charles Brower, Alex McCain, Clarence Nichols, George Robinson, Walter Ellerbe (World War II veteran), John Ellerbe, Jimmy Ellerbe (Vietnam War hero killed in battle), John Ingram, Jesse Scott, Jesse Thompson (The men of Ellerbe Grove Missionary Baptist Church).

Do you know a black man from a bygone era who should be included in this list? This book also is dedicated to him.

———————————————————————

About the Cover

The cover is an original work done by artist Ron Crawford of Charlotte, N.C. He has produced works for The Charlotte Oserver and as a motor sports artist where he has done of NASCAR drivers.

If you would like a larger print of this book design, please send email to cmach4@carolina.rr.com.